AI MADE EASY: A BEGINNER'S GUIDE TO ARTIFICIAL INTELLIGENCE

AI For Beginners

Asif Mehmood

CONTENTS

CHAPTER 1:
INTRODUCTION TO AI

Artificial Intelligence, or AI, is a concept that has captured the imagination of many and is transforming the world as we know it. At its core, AI refers to the simulation of human intelligence in machines, enabling them to perform tasks that typically require human intelligence, such as understanding natural language, recognizing patterns, learning from experience, and making decisions. This chapter serves as an entry point into the fascinating world of AI, providing readers with a foundational understanding of its principles and significance.

To begin, let's delve into the definition of AI. In its simplest form, AI encompasses the development of computer systems that can perform tasks that would normally require human intelligence. These tasks can range from basic functions like recognizing speech or images to more complex activities such as driving autonomous vehicles or diagnosing medical conditions. AI systems achieve these feats through a combination of algorithms, data, and computational power, mimicking the cognitive abilities of the human brain.

The history of AI is rich and storied, dating back to ancient times with myths and legends of artificial beings capable of independent thought. However, the modern era of AI began in the 1950s, with the groundbreaking work of pioneers like Alan Turing and John McCarthy. Since then, AI has evolved rapidly, driven by advances in computer technology, algorithms, and the availability of vast amounts of data. Key milestones in AI development, such as the creation of expert systems, neural networks, and deep learning algorithms, have paved the way for the transformative applications of AI that we see today.

But why does AI matter? The significance of AI lies in its ability to augment human capabilities, improve efficiency, and solve complex problems across various domains. In healthcare, AI is revolutionizing diagnostics and treatment planning, helping doctors make more accurate diagnoses and personalize patient care. In finance, AI-powered algorithms are optimizing trading strategies, detecting fraudulent activities, and providing personalized financial advice to consumers. In transportation, AI is driving the development of autonomous vehicles, reducing accidents, and enhancing the efficiency of transportation networks.

Moreover, AI has permeated into our daily lives, shaping how we interact with technology and the world around us. From virtual assistants like Siri and Alexa to recommendation systems on streaming platforms like Netflix, AI-powered technologies have become integral parts of our digital ecosystem.

As we embark on this journey into the realm of AI, it's essential to recognize the vast potential and profound impact that AI holds for society. While the possibilities are endless, so too are the challenges and ethical considerations that accompany AI development and deployment. From concerns about job displacement to issues of algorithmic bias and privacy, navigating the ethical complexities of AI requires careful consideration and proactive measures to ensure that AI technologies are developed and used responsibly.

Definition Of Ai:

Artificial Intelligence (AI) refers to the development of computer systems that can perform tasks that typically require human intelligence. These tasks include understanding natural language, recognizing patterns, learning from experience, and making decisions based on that learning. AI systems are designed to mimic cognitive functions such as problem-solving, perception, reasoning, and learning, enabling them to interact with the environment and adapt to changing circumstances.

AI encompasses a wide range of techniques and approaches, including machine learning, neural networks, deep learning, natural language processing, computer vision, and robotics. These technologies enable AI systems to analyze large volumes of data, identify patterns, and make predictions or decisions autonomously.

In today's world, AI is ubiquitous, powering many of the technologies and services we use daily, from virtual assistants and recommendation systems to autonomous vehicles and medical diagnostics. Its significance lies in its ability to augment human capabilities, improve efficiency, and solve complex problems across various domains, revolutionizing industries and transforming the way we live, work, and interact with technology.

Brief History:

The history of AI can be traced back to ancient times, with myths and legends depicting artificial beings capable of independent thought. However, the modern era of AI began in the 1950s, marked by significant milestones and breakthroughs:

- **1950s:** The birth of AI as a field of study is often credited to the seminal work of Alan Turing, who proposed the Turing Test as a measure of a machine's intelligence. Other key figures of this era include John McCarthy, who coined the term "artificial intelligence" and organized the first AI conference at Dartmouth College in 1956.

- **1960s-1970s:** The development of expert systems, which are AI systems designed to mimic the decision-making abilities of human experts in specific domains, marked this period. Programs like DENDRAL and MYCIN demonstrated the potential of AI in tasks such as chemical analysis and medical diagnosis.

- **1980s-1990s:** The focus shifted to machine learning and neural networks, with advancements in algorithms and computing power driving progress in AI research. The development of backpropagation, a technique for training neural networks, and the resurgence of interest in neural network research laid the groundwork for future breakthroughs in AI.

- **2000s-Present:** The rise of big data and the advent of deep learning revolutionized AI, enabling the training of large-scale neural networks on massive datasets. Breakthroughs in areas such as computer vision, natural language processing, and reinforcement learning have led to the development of AI systems capable of human-level performance in tasks such as image recognition, language translation, and game playing.

Why Ai Matters:

AI plays a crucial role in various industries and everyday life, offering numerous benefits and opportunities:

- **Healthcare:** AI is revolutionizing healthcare by improving diagnostics, personalized treatment planning, drug discovery, and patient care management. AI-powered systems can analyze medical images, detect diseases at an early stage, and recommend optimal treatment strategies, leading to better patient outcomes and reduced healthcare costs.

- **Finance:** In the financial sector, AI is used for fraud detection, algorithmic trading, risk assessment, customer service automation, and personalized financial advice. AI-powered algorithms can analyze vast amounts of financial data in real-time, identify suspicious activities, and make data-driven investment decisions, enhancing efficiency and reducing risks for financial institutions and consumers.

- **Transportation:** AI is driving innovation in transportation, with applications ranging from autonomous vehicles and traffic management systems to predictive maintenance and route optimization. AI-powered technologies can improve road safety, reduce traffic congestion, and enhance the efficiency of transportation networks, leading to smoother and more sustainable urban mobility solutions.

- **Entertainment:** AI is reshaping the entertainment industry by personalizing content recommendations, generating creative content, and enhancing user experiences. AI-powered recommendation systems can analyze user preferences and behaviors to recommend movies, music, and other content tailored to individual tastes, while AI-driven content creation tools can assist artists and creators in generating music, art, and literature.

In addition to these industries, AI has broader implications for society, economy, and governance, shaping how we work, communicate, and interact with technology. Its transformative potential extends to areas such as education, agriculture, manufacturing, environmental sustainability, and national security, driving innovation, economic growth, and social progress.

In summary, AI matters because it holds the promise of solving some of the most pressing challenges facing humanity, improving the quality of life, and unlocking new opportunities for innovation and progress across various domains. Its impact on society and the economy is profound, making it a key driver of technological advancement and societal transformation in the 21st century.

◆ ◆ ◆

CHAPTER 2: UNDERSTANDING AI CONCEPTS

I n this chapter, we'll delve deeper into the fundamental concepts of artificial intelligence (AI), focusing on different types of AI, the role of machine learning, the significance of deep learning, and the basics of neural networks.

Types Of Ai: Narrow Ai Vs. General Ai

AI can be categorized into two main types: Narrow AI (Weak AI) and General AI (Strong AI).

- **Narrow AI:** Narrow AI refers to AI systems that are designed and trained for a specific task or set of tasks. These systems excel at performing well-defined tasks within a limited domain. Examples of narrow AI include virtual assistants like Siri and Alexa, image recognition systems, recommendation algorithms, and autonomous vehicles. Narrow AI systems are prevalent in today's world and have demonstrated remarkable capabilities in various applications.

- **General AI:** General AI, also known as Artificial General

Intelligence (AGI) or Strong AI, refers to AI systems that possess human-like intelligence and can perform any intellectual task that a human being can. Unlike narrow AI, which is specialized in specific domains, general AI would have the ability to understand, learn, and apply knowledge across a wide range of tasks and contexts. Achieving general AI remains a long-term goal of AI research and is still largely theoretical.

Machine Learning:

Machine learning is a subset of AI that focuses on the development of algorithms and statistical models that enable computers to learn from and make predictions or decisions based on data. The core idea behind machine learning is to enable computers to learn from experience, without being explicitly programmed for specific tasks.

Machine learning algorithms can be broadly categorized into three types:

- **Supervised Learning:** In supervised learning, the algorithm is trained on labeled data, where each input is associated with a corresponding output. The algorithm learns to map inputs to outputs by identifying patterns and relationships in the training data. Examples of supervised learning tasks include classification (e.g., spam detection, image recognition) and regression (e.g., predicting house prices, estimating sales revenue).

- **Unsupervised Learning:** In unsupervised learning, the algorithm is trained on unlabeled data, and its objective is to uncover hidden patterns or structures within the data. Unsupervised learning algorithms cluster similar data points together or reduce the dimensionality of the data to reveal underlying relationships. Examples of unsupervised learning tasks include clustering (e.g., customer segmentation, document categorization) and dimensionality reduction (e.g., principal component analysis).

- **Reinforcement Learning:** In reinforcement learning, the algorithm learns to interact with an environment in order to maximize a cumulative reward. The algorithm learns through trial and error, receiving feedback from the environment in the form of rewards or penalties for its actions. Reinforcement learning is used in applications such as game playing, robotics, and autonomous vehicle navigation.

Machine learning techniques have been instrumental in enabling AI systems to perform complex tasks such as natural language processing, computer vision, and autonomous decision-making.

Deep Learning:

Deep learning is a subset of machine learning that focuses on training deep neural networks, which are artificial neural networks with multiple layers of interconnected nodes (neurons). Deep learning algorithms are inspired by the structure and functioning of the human brain and are capable of learning hierarchical representations of data.

Deep learning has revolutionized AI research and applications, particularly in areas such as image recognition, speech recognition, natural language processing, and generative modeling. Deep neural networks can automatically extract features from raw data, learn complex patterns, and make predictions or decisions with high accuracy.

Examples of deep learning architectures include convolutional neural networks (CNNs) for image recognition, recurrent neural networks (RNNs) for sequential data processing (e.g., speech recognition, language translation), and generative adversarial networks (GANs) for generating realistic synthetic data.

Neural Networks:

Neural networks are computational models inspired by the structure and functioning of biological neural networks in the human brain. A neural network consists of interconnected nodes, or neurons, organized into layers. Each neuron receives input signals, processes them through an activation function, and produces an output signal, which is then passed on to the next layer of neurons.

The basic building blocks of a neural network are:

- **Input Layer:** The input layer receives the initial input data and passes it to the next layer of neurons.

- **Hidden Layers:** Hidden layers are intermediate layers of neurons between the input and output layers. Each neuron in a hidden layer receives input from the previous layer, processes it through an activation function, and passes the result to the next layer.

- **Output Layer:** The output layer produces the final output of the neural network, which could be a classification label, a regression value, or a probability distribution.

During the training process, a neural network learns to adjust its weights and biases through a process called backpropagation, where errors in the output are propagated backward through the network to update the parameters and minimize the difference between the predicted and actual outputs.

Neural networks are highly flexible and can be used to model complex relationships in data, making them well-suited for a wide range of AI tasks, including pattern recognition, classification, regression, and sequence prediction.

In summary, understanding the concepts of AI, including different types of AI, machine learning, deep learning, and neural networks, lays the foundation for exploring the capabilities and applications of AI in various domains. These concepts provide the building blocks for developing intelligent systems that can learn from data, make informed decisions, and adapt to changing environments, driving innovation and progress in the field of artificial intelligence.

CHAPTER 3:
APPLICATIONS OF AI

A rtificial intelligence (AI) is transforming various industries, revolutionizing the way we work, interact, and live. In this chapter, we'll explore some of the most impactful applications of AI across different sectors, including healthcare, finance, transportation, and entertainment.

Ai In Healthcare:

The healthcare industry is undergoing a significant transformation fueled by advancements in AI technology. AI is being leveraged to improve patient care, optimize medical processes, and accelerate scientific research. Some key applications of AI in healthcare include:

- **Medical Imaging Analysis:** AI-powered algorithms can analyze medical images, such as X-rays, MRIs, and CT scans, to detect abnormalities and assist radiologists in diagnosis. Deep learning techniques have demonstrated remarkable accuracy in identifying and classifying diseases, such as cancerous tumors and fractures, leading to earlier detection and improved patient outcomes.

- **Personalized Treatment Recommendations:** AI-driven platforms can analyze patient data, including medical records, genetic information, and lifestyle factors, to generate personalized treatment plans and recommendations. By tailoring treatment strategies to individual patient profiles, AI can improve treatment efficacy, reduce adverse effects, and enhance patient satisfaction.

- **Drug Discovery and Development:** AI algorithms are being used to accelerate the drug discovery process by analyzing vast amounts of biological data, identifying potential drug candidates, and predicting their efficacy and safety profiles. AI-powered drug discovery platforms have the potential to streamline the drug development pipeline, reduce costs, and bring new therapies to market faster.

Ai In Finance:

In the financial services industry, AI is driving innovation and efficiency across various functions, from risk management and fraud detection to customer service and investment management. Some key applications of AI in finance include:

- **Fraud Detection:** AI algorithms can analyze transaction data in real-time to detect suspicious activities and identify fraudulent transactions. Machine learning models can learn from historical data to recognize patterns of fraudulent behavior and flag potentially fraudulent transactions for further investigation, helping financial institutions mitigate risks and protect against financial fraud.

- **Algorithmic Trading:** AI-powered trading algorithms

can analyze market data, identify trading opportunities, and execute trades autonomously with minimal human intervention. Machine learning models can learn from historical market data to identify patterns and trends, optimize trading strategies, and adapt to changing market conditions in real-time, leading to improved trading performance and higher returns on investment.

- **Customer Service Automation:** AI-powered chatbots and virtual assistants are transforming customer service in the finance industry, enabling financial institutions to provide personalized, round-the-clock support to customers. Natural language processing (NLP) algorithms can understand customer inquiries, answer questions, and perform transactions, reducing wait times, improving service quality, and enhancing the overall customer experience.

Ai In Transportation:

The transportation industry is embracing AI to improve safety, efficiency, and sustainability across various modes of transportation. Some key applications of AI in transportation include:

- **Autonomous Vehicles:** AI-powered autonomous vehicles are revolutionizing the way we travel, offering the potential to reduce accidents, congestion, and emissions while increasing mobility and accessibility. Self-driving cars use a combination of sensors, cameras, and AI algorithms to perceive the environment, navigate complex road conditions, and make real-time driving decisions without human intervention.

- **Traffic Management Systems:** AI algorithms are being

used to optimize traffic flow, reduce congestion, and improve transportation efficiency in urban areas. Traffic management systems can analyze real-time traffic data from sensors, cameras, and GPS devices to identify traffic bottlenecks, predict congestion patterns, and dynamically adjust traffic signals and routing to optimize traffic flow and minimize travel time.

Ai In Entertainment:

In the entertainment industry, AI is reshaping how content is created, curated, and consumed, enhancing entertainment experiences for audiences worldwide. Some key applications of AI in entertainment include:

- **Recommendation Systems:** AI-powered recommendation algorithms analyze user preferences, behavior, and viewing history to personalize content recommendations on streaming platforms, music services, and e-commerce websites. By suggesting relevant content based on individual tastes and preferences, recommendation systems can improve user engagement, retention, and satisfaction.

- **Content Creation:** AI algorithms are being used to generate creative content, such as music, art, and literature, autonomously or in collaboration with human creators. Generative AI models can learn from existing examples and create new content that mimics the style, structure, and themes of the original works, enabling artists and creators to explore new creative possibilities and push the boundaries of artistic expression.

- **Virtual Assistants:** AI-powered virtual assistants,

such as chatbots and voice-activated assistants, are enhancing user interactions and customer service in the entertainment industry. Virtual assistants can answer customer inquiries, provide personalized recommendations, and assist with booking tickets, reservations, and purchases, improving customer engagement and satisfaction.

CHAPTER 4: ETHICS AND IMPLICATIONS OF AI

A rtificial intelligence (AI) holds immense promise for improving our lives, but it also presents significant ethical and societal challenges. In this chapter, we'll examine the ethical considerations, regulatory frameworks, and social impact of AI, exploring the implications of this powerful technology on individuals, communities, and societies at large.

Ethical Considerations:

AI systems are not immune to bias, discrimination, and unintended consequences, raising important ethical questions that must be addressed. Some key ethical considerations surrounding AI include:

- **Bias in Algorithms:** AI algorithms can reflect and perpetuate biases present in the data used to train them, leading to discriminatory outcomes in areas such as hiring, lending, and criminal justice. Addressing algorithmic bias requires careful attention to data quality, transparency, and fairness throughout the AI development lifecycle.

- **Privacy Concerns:** AI systems often rely on vast amounts of personal data to make predictions and recommendations, raising concerns about privacy and data protection. Unauthorized access, misuse, or mishandling of sensitive data can infringe on individuals' privacy rights and undermine trust in AI technologies.

- **Job Displacement:** The automation of tasks and roles traditionally performed by humans can lead to job displacement and economic dislocation, particularly in industries heavily impacted by AI technologies. Ensuring a just transition for workers affected by automation requires proactive measures such as reskilling, upskilling, and social safety nets to mitigate the negative impact on employment and livelihoods.

Regulatory Frameworks:

Governments and regulatory bodies are grappling with the need to develop comprehensive frameworks to govern the development and deployment of AI technologies. Some key areas of focus include:

- **Data Governance:** Regulations governing data collection, storage, and use are essential for protecting individuals' privacy and ensuring responsible data practices. Data protection laws such as the General Data Protection Regulation (GDPR) in Europe and the California Consumer Privacy Act (CCPA) in the United States set standards for data privacy and security, with implications for AI applications that rely on personal data.

- **Algorithmic Accountability:** Regulatory frameworks are needed to hold AI developers and users accountable for the impact of their algorithms on individuals and society. Measures such as algorithmic transparency, explainability, and auditability can help identify and mitigate biases, errors, and unintended consequences in AI systems.

- **Ethical Guidelines:** Ethical guidelines and principles for AI development and deployment can provide a framework for responsible AI innovation. Initiatives such as the IEEE Global Initiative on Ethics of Autonomous and Intelligent Systems and the Partnership on AI offer principles and guidelines to promote ethical AI practices and address societal concerns.

Social Impact:

The widespread adoption of AI technologies has far-reaching implications for society, shaping how we work, communicate, and interact with technology. Some key social impacts of AI include:

- **Exacerbation of Inequality:** AI has the potential to exacerbate existing inequalities, widening the gap between those who have access to AI technologies and those who do not. Issues such as algorithmic bias, digital divide, and unequal access to AI-driven opportunities can deepen social disparities and exacerbate systemic inequities.

- **Economic Disruption:** The automation of jobs and tasks by AI technologies can disrupt labor markets and reshape economies, leading to shifts in employment patterns, income distribution, and skills demand.

Ensuring inclusive economic growth and equitable distribution of the benefits of AI requires proactive policies and investments in education, training, and social support systems.

- **Ethical Decision-Making:** AI systems are increasingly being tasked with making ethical decisions that have profound implications for individuals and society. From autonomous vehicles deciding who to prioritize in life-threatening situations to AI-powered healthcare systems determining treatment options, ethical considerations must be embedded into AI design and decision-making processes to ensure alignment with societal values and norms.

In conclusion, the ethical and societal implications of AI are complex and multifaceted, requiring interdisciplinary collaboration, stakeholder engagement, and proactive governance to address. By promoting ethical AI practices, fostering regulatory oversight, and mitigating the social impacts of AI, we can harness the transformative potential of this technology while safeguarding the interests and values of individuals and communities.

◆ ◆ ◆

CHAPTER 5: GETTING STARTED WITH AI

Embarking on a journey into the realm of artificial intelligence (AI) can be both exciting and daunting, especially for beginners. In this chapter, we'll explore various resources, tools, and practical steps to help you get started with AI and machine learning.

Learning Resources:

Here are some recommended online courses, tutorials, and books for beginners interested in learning about AI:

- **Online Courses:**
    - Coursera: "AI For Everyone" by Andrew Ng - An accessible introduction to AI concepts and applications for non-technical audiences.
    - Udacity: "Intro to Artificial Intelligence" - A beginner-friendly course covering key AI topics such as search algorithms, machine learning, and neural networks.
    - edX: "Introduction to Artificial Intelligence (AI)" - A comprehensive introduction to AI principles and techniques, taught by leading experts in the field.

- **Tutorials:**
  - TensorFlow Tutorials - TensorFlow provides a wealth of tutorials and guides for learning about machine learning and deep learning using its open-source framework.
  - PyTorch Tutorials - PyTorch offers tutorials and documentation for beginners looking to learn about deep learning and neural networks.
- **Books:**
  - "Artificial Intelligence: A Guide for Thinking Humans" by Melanie Mitchell - A thought-provoking exploration of AI concepts and their implications for society, written for a general audience.
  - "Hands-On Machine Learning with Scikit-Learn, Keras, and TensorFlow" by Aurélien Géron - A practical guide to machine learning and deep learning techniques, with hands-on examples and exercises for beginners.

Tools And Platforms:

Here are some beginner-friendly tools and platforms for experimenting with AI and machine learning projects:

- **Google Colab:** Google Colab is a free, cloud-based platform that provides access to GPUs and TPUs for running machine learning experiments. It supports popular libraries such as TensorFlow and PyTorch and offers pre-installed packages for data analysis and visualization.
- **TensorFlow Playground:** TensorFlow Playground is an interactive web-based tool that allows users to experiment with neural networks in a visual environment. It's a great way for beginners to

learn about neural networks and explore different architectures and parameters.

- **IBM Watson Studio:** IBM Watson Studio is a comprehensive platform for data science and AI development, offering tools for data preparation, model development, and deployment. It provides a user-friendly interface and supports collaboration and integration with other IBM Watson services.

- **Microsoft Azure AI:** Microsoft Azure offers a suite of AI services and tools for building, training, and deploying AI models. Azure Machine Learning Studio provides a drag-and-drop interface for building machine learning pipelines, while Azure Notebooks allows users to run Python code in a cloud-based environment.

Building Your First Ai Project:

Now that you have some foundational knowledge and tools at your disposal, let's walk through the steps of creating a simple AI project, such as a chatbot or image classifier:

1. **Define Your Project:** Decide on the scope and objectives of your project. For example, if you're building a chatbot, determine what tasks it will perform and what questions it will answer.

2. **Gather Data:** Collect and prepare the data you'll need to train your AI model. For a chatbot, this could include a dataset of questions and answers, while for an image classifier, you'll need a dataset of labeled images.

3. **Choose a Framework:** Select a machine learning framework or library to build your AI model. TensorFlow and PyTorch are popular choices for deep learning projects, while scikit-learn is a great option for traditional machine learning tasks.

4. **Train Your Model:** Use your chosen framework to train your AI model on the prepared data. Experiment with different architectures, parameters, and hyperparameters to optimize performance.

5. **Evaluate Your Model:** Evaluate the performance of your trained model using metrics such as accuracy, precision, recall, and F1 score. Identify areas for improvement and fine-tune your model as needed.

6. **Deploy Your Model:** Once you're satisfied with the performance of your model, deploy it to a production environment where it can be used in real-world applications. This could involve integrating your model into a web application, mobile app, or other software system.

7. **Monitor and Iterate:** Continuously monitor the performance of your deployed model and gather feedback from users. Iterate on your model based on feedback and new data to improve its accuracy and effectiveness over time.

By following these steps, you can build and deploy your first AI project and gain hands-on experience with AI development. Remember to start small, experiment, and don't be afraid to make mistakes – learning from failure is an essential part of the AI journey.

◆ ◆ ◆

CHAPTER 6: THE FUTURE OF AI

As artificial intelligence (AI) continues to evolve at a rapid pace, the future holds immense promise for transformative advancements across various domains. In this chapter, we'll explore emerging trends, challenges, opportunities, and the importance of ethical considerations in shaping the future of AI.

Emerging Trends:

Several emerging trends are shaping the landscape of AI and driving innovation in the field:

- **Reinforcement Learning:** Reinforcement learning, a branch of machine learning focused on learning from feedback and rewards, is gaining traction for its ability to solve complex decision-making tasks in dynamic environments. Applications of reinforcement learning span autonomous robotics, gaming, finance, and healthcare, with potential for breakthroughs in areas such as self-driving cars and personalized medicine.

- **Natural Language Processing (NLP) Advancements:** Recent advancements in natural language processing, fueled by deep learning techniques and large-scale language models, are enabling AI systems to understand and generate human language with unprecedented accuracy and fluency. NLP applications range from virtual assistants and chatbots to language translation, sentiment analysis, and content generation.

- **AI-Driven Creativity:** AI technologies are increasingly being used to augment human creativity and artistic expression across various domains, including music, art, literature, and design. Generative AI models, such as GANs and neural style transfer, can generate realistic images, compose music, write poetry, and create visual artworks, blurring the lines between human and machine creativity.

Challenges And Opportunities:

While AI presents significant opportunities for innovation and growth, it also poses several challenges that must be addressed:

- **Ethical and Social Implications:** The widespread adoption of AI raises ethical concerns related to privacy, bias, accountability, and societal impact. Ensuring that AI systems are developed and deployed responsibly requires proactive measures to address these ethical considerations and mitigate potential harms.

- **AI Safety and Robustness:** Ensuring the safety and reliability of AI systems is crucial to their widespread adoption and acceptance. Challenges such as adversarial attacks, robustness to distributional shifts, and unintended consequences pose significant obstacles to achieving AI safety and require research and development efforts to overcome.

- **Workforce Displacement and Reskilling:** The automation of tasks by AI technologies has the potential to disrupt labor markets and lead to job displacement in certain industries. Addressing the impact of AI on employment requires proactive measures such as reskilling, upskilling, and workforce development initiatives to prepare individuals for the jobs of the future.

Ethical Ai:

Developing ethical AI systems is paramount to ensuring that AI technologies benefit society and align with human values and norms. Individuals, organizations, and policymakers all have a role to play in shaping the future of AI responsibly:

- **Transparency and Accountability:** AI developers should prioritize transparency and accountability in the design, development, and deployment of AI systems. Providing explanations for AI decisions, disclosing data sources and biases, and establishing mechanisms for oversight and accountability are essential for building trust and ensuring ethical AI practices.

- **Fairness and Bias Mitigation:** Addressing bias and promoting fairness in AI algorithms and systems is critical to preventing discrimination and promoting equality. Techniques such as algorithmic auditing, bias detection, and fairness-aware machine learning can help mitigate biases and ensure equitable outcomes for diverse populations.

- **Human-Centered Design:** Prioritizing human values, needs, and preferences in AI design and development is essential for creating AI systems that enhance human well-being and autonomy. Human-centered design principles, such as user engagement, inclusivity, and accessibility, should guide the development of AI technologies to ensure that they serve the best interests of humanity.

CHAPTER 7: PRACTICAL APPLICATIONS OF AI IN BUSINESS

U nderstanding AI Analytics

In today's data-driven business landscape, AI analytics are proving to be indispensable tools for organizations seeking to gain actionable insights from vast amounts of data. AI-powered analytics go beyond traditional business intelligence by leveraging advanced algorithms and machine learning techniques to uncover hidden patterns, trends, and correlations in data. Predictive modeling, for example, allows businesses to forecast future trends and behaviors based on historical data, enabling more informed decision-making and strategic planning. Similarly, prescriptive analytics provides recommendations for optimizing business processes and achieving specific outcomes, guiding organizations towards greater efficiency and effectiveness.

Enhancing Customer Segmentation

AI-driven customer segmentation is revolutionizing marketing strategies by enabling businesses to divide their customer base into distinct segments based on demographics, behavior, and preferences. This allows for more targeted and personalized marketing campaigns, tailored product recommendations, and customized communication strategies. By understanding the unique needs and preferences of different customer segments, businesses can deliver more relevant and engaging experiences, leading to higher levels of customer satisfaction and loyalty.

Optimizing Supply Chains

AI is reshaping supply chain management by enabling organizations to optimize inventory levels, predict demand fluctuations, and identify inefficiencies in their operations. AI algorithms analyze vast amounts of data from various sources, such as sales data, production schedules, and supplier information, to identify patterns and trends that can inform decision-making. By accurately predicting demand and optimizing inventory levels, businesses can reduce stockouts, minimize excess inventory, and improve overall supply chain efficiency. Additionally, AI-powered predictive maintenance systems help organizations identify equipment failures before they occur, reducing downtime and increasing operational reliability.

Personalizing Marketing Campaigns

AI-powered marketing tools are transforming how businesses engage with their customers by delivering personalized and relevant marketing campaigns. By analyzing customer data, such as purchase history, browsing behavior, and social media interactions, AI algorithms can segment customers into distinct groups and deliver targeted messaging and offers. This personalized approach enhances customer engagement, increases conversion rates, and ultimately drives revenue growth. Moreover, AI-driven recommendation engines can suggest products or services based on individual preferences, further enhancing the customer experience and fostering brand loyalty.

In summary, AI is revolutionizing business operations by enabling organizations to leverage data-driven insights, enhance customer engagement, and optimize processes across various domains. By embracing AI technologies and integrating them into their operations, businesses can gain a competitive edge and drive sustainable growth in today's dynamic marketplace.

CHAPTER 8: AI IN EDUCATION AND TRAINING

Personalized Learning Platforms

AI-powered adaptive learning platforms are revolutionizing education by providing personalized learning experiences tailored to each student's needs and preferences. These platforms use machine learning algorithms to analyze student performance data and deliver customized instruction and support. By adapting the pace, content, and format of instruction to individual learning styles, adaptive learning platforms help students master difficult concepts, overcome learning challenges, and achieve academic success.

Adaptive Tutoring Systems

AI tutors provide personalized instruction and support to students, offering real-time feedback, hints, and explanations to help them master difficult concepts. By analyzing student responses and interactions, AI tutors can identify areas of weakness and provide targeted interventions to address learning gaps. This individualized approach enhances student engagement, promotes self-directed learning, and improves academic outcomes.

Creating Interactive Educational Content

AI technologies generate interactive educational content such as quizzes, tutorials, and simulations, enhancing engagement and comprehension. These tools leverage natural language processing (NLP) and machine learning algorithms to create dynamic and interactive learning experiences. By providing hands-on practice and immediate feedback, interactive educational content reinforces key concepts and promotes deeper learning.

Professional Development For Educators

AI-powered coaching and mentoring systems support teacher professional development by analyzing teaching practices, providing feedback, and offering personalized recommendations for growth and improvement. These systems help educators refine their instructional strategies, adapt to the needs of diverse learners, and stay abreast of the latest pedagogical trends and best practices. By empowering educators with personalized support and resources, AI technologies contribute to the continuous improvement of teaching quality and student learning outcomes.

In conclusion, AI is transforming education and training by personalizing learning experiences, improving instructional quality, and empowering educators to excel in their profession. By leveraging AI technologies, educational institutions and training organizations can create more effective, engaging, and equitable learning environments that meet the needs of all learners.

CHAPTER 9: AI FOR HEALTHCARE INNOVATION

Medical Imaging Analysis

AI algorithms analyze medical images with unprecedented accuracy, assisting clinicians in diagnosing diseases and guiding treatment decisions. By automating image interpretation tasks, AI technologies help radiologists identify abnormalities, detect early signs of disease, and assess treatment response. This leads to earlier detection, more accurate diagnosis, and improved patient outcomes across a wide range of medical specialties.

Predictive Analytics And Clinical Decision Support

AI-powered predictive analytics leverage patient data to predict disease progression and recommend personalized treatment plans. By analyzing electronic health records (EHRs), genomic data, and other patient information, AI algorithms identify patterns and trends that can inform clinical decision-making. This enables clinicians to deliver proactive and personalized care, optimize treatment strategies, and improve patient outcomes.

Accelerating Drug Discovery And Development

AI accelerates drug discovery by analyzing large-scale biological data and identifying potential drug targets. By leveraging machine learning algorithms and computational modeling techniques, AI technologies help pharmaceutical companies identify promising drug candidates, predict their efficacy and safety profiles, and optimize their chemical structures. This leads to the development of novel therapies with enhanced therapeutic benefits and reduced side effects, benefiting patients worldwide.

Improving Healthcare Operations

AI optimizes healthcare operations by automating administrative tasks, predicting patient flow, and optimizing resource allocation. By analyzing data from electronic health records (EHRs), hospital systems, and other sources, AI algorithms identify inefficiencies, streamline workflows, and improve the delivery of care. This leads to reduced costs, increased efficiency, and enhanced patient satisfaction across the healthcare continuum.

In summary, AI is revolutionizing healthcare by enabling earlier detection, more accurate diagnosis, and personalized treatment. By leveraging AI technologies, healthcare providers can improve patient outcomes, enhance clinical decision-making, and transform the delivery of care in today's complex and rapidly evolving healthcare landscape.

◆ ◆ ◆

CHAPTER 10: AI AND SUSTAINABILITY

Environmental Monitoring and Conservation
AI technologies play a crucial role in environmental monitoring and conservation efforts by enabling real-time analysis of environmental data. Remote sensing techniques combined with AI algorithms allow for the monitoring of ecosystems, wildlife habitats, and natural resources. By analyzing satellite imagery, sensor data, and other environmental data sources, AI can detect changes in land use, deforestation, and wildlife populations, providing valuable insights for conservation initiatives. Moreover, AI-powered predictive models can forecast environmental trends and inform decision-making processes aimed at preserving biodiversity and mitigating the impacts of climate change.

Precision Agriculture

AI-driven precision agriculture techniques optimize crop production while minimizing environmental impact. By integrating data from sensors, drones, and satellite imagery, AI algorithms can monitor soil conditions, crop health, and weather patterns in real-time. This data-driven approach enables farmers to make informed decisions about planting, irrigation, fertilization, and pest management, resulting in higher yields, reduced resource usage, and decreased environmental footprint. Precision agriculture not only enhances agricultural productivity but also promotes sustainability by conserving water, reducing chemical inputs, and preserving soil health.

Renewable Energy Optimization

AI plays a critical role in optimizing the generation, distribution, and consumption of renewable energy sources such as solar and wind power. AI algorithms analyze data from weather forecasts, energy markets, and power grid operations to optimize the deployment of renewable energy resources. By predicting energy demand, optimizing energy storage, and balancing supply and demand in real-time, AI helps maximize the efficiency and reliability of renewable energy systems. This enables the integration of renewable energy sources into the grid, reduces reliance on fossil fuels, and accelerates the transition to a sustainable energy future.

Smart Grid Management

AI-powered smart grid technologies improve the efficiency and reliability of energy distribution systems. By analyzing data from smart meters, sensors, and IoT devices, AI algorithms can detect anomalies, predict equipment failures, and optimize grid operations. This proactive approach to grid management reduces the risk of power outages, minimizes energy losses, and improves overall grid stability. Moreover, AI facilitates the integration of distributed energy resources such as solar panels and electric vehicles, enabling more efficient use of renewable energy and reducing greenhouse gas emissions.

In summary, AI technologies have the potential to drive sustainable development by optimizing resource management, conserving biodiversity, and mitigating the impacts of climate change. By harnessing the power of AI, governments, businesses, and communities can work towards a more sustainable future for generations to come.

CHAPTER 11: AI ETHICS IN PRACTICE

Transparency and Accountability

Ethical AI development requires transparency and accountability throughout the AI lifecycle. Organizations must disclose data sources, algorithms, and decision-making processes to ensure transparency and enable accountability for AI outcomes. By providing insights into how AI systems work and how decisions are made, transparency builds trust and fosters responsible AI practices.

Fairness And Bias Mitigation

Addressing bias in AI algorithms is critical to ensuring fairness and equity in decision-making processes. AI developers must employ techniques such as algorithmic auditing, bias detection, and fairness-aware machine learning to identify and mitigate biases. By promoting fairness and reducing discrimination, organizations can build more inclusive and equitable AI systems that benefit all individuals and communities.

Human-Centered Design

AI systems should prioritize human values, needs, and

preferences in their design and development. Human-centered design principles emphasize user engagement, inclusivity, and accessibility, ensuring that AI technologies serve the best interests of humanity. By considering the impact of AI on diverse stakeholders and designing solutions that address their needs, organizations can create more ethical and socially responsible AI systems.

Responsible Ai Governance

Governments, regulatory bodies, and industry stakeholders play a crucial role in shaping the governance and regulation of AI. Establishing ethical guidelines, standards, and oversight mechanisms is essential to promote responsible AI development and deployment. By implementing policies that prioritize ethical considerations and protect public interests, policymakers can ensure that AI technologies benefit society while minimizing risks and harms

CHAPTER 12: AI GOVERNANCE AND REGULATION

Data Privacy Regulations
Data privacy regulations govern the collection, use, and sharing of personal data in AI systems. Compliance with regulations such as the General Data Protection Regulation (GDPR) and the California Consumer Privacy Act (CCPA) is essential to protect individuals' privacy rights and ensure responsible data practices. Organizations must implement robust data protection measures, obtain consent for data processing activities, and provide individuals with control over their personal information to comply with these regulations.

Algorithmic Transparency Requirements

Regulations may require AI developers to provide transparency into their algorithms and decision-making processes. This promotes accountability and enables stakeholders to understand how AI systems work and how decisions are made. By disclosing information about data sources, model architecture, and decision criteria, organizations can build trust and ensure transparency in their AI systems.

Liability And Accountability Frameworks

Establishing liability and accountability frameworks is crucial to address the potential risks and harms associated with AI technologies. Clarifying roles and responsibilities helps mitigate legal and ethical concerns and ensures that AI developers are held accountable for their actions. Organizations must assess and mitigate risks, establish mechanisms for redress and compensation, and allocate liability appropriately to promote responsible AI development and deployment.

Ethical Guidelines For Ai Research And Development

Developing ethical guidelines for AI research and development promotes responsible innovation and ethical AI practices. These guidelines address issues such as bias mitigation, fairness, transparency, and human rights, guiding AI developers in creating technologies that benefit society while minimizing risks and harms. By adhering to ethical principles and best practices, organizations can ensure that AI technologies are developed and deployed in a manner that upholds ethical standards and societal values.

In summary, governance and regulation are essential to promote responsible AI development and deployment. By implementing data privacy regulations, transparency requirements, liability frameworks, and ethical guidelines, policymakers can create an enabling environment for AI innovation while protecting individuals' rights and promoting the public interest. Collaborative efforts between governments, regulatory bodies, industry stakeholders, and civil society are essential to address the complex challenges and opportunities posed by AI technologies and ensure that AI benefits society as a whole.

In conclusion, the potential of AI to revolutionize every aspect of our lives is immense. From enhancing business operations and improving educational outcomes to advancing healthcare innovation and promoting environmental sustainability, AI holds the promise of transforming our world for the better.

As we continue to explore the practical applications, ethical considerations, and governance frameworks surrounding AI, it becomes increasingly clear that the responsible development and deployment of AI technologies are essential. By harnessing the power of AI for good, we can address some of the most pressing challenges facing humanity and unlock new opportunities for innovation, growth, and prosperity.

Ultimately, the question is not whether AI can help us, but how much AI can help us. With careful stewardship, collaboration, and a commitment to ethical principles, we can harness the transformative potential of AI to build a brighter, more inclusive, and sustainable future for generations to come.